Whispers of Strength: Poetic Journey Through Resilience and Healing

Aisse Magassa

BookLeaf Publishing

India | USA | UK

Presentation by *BookLeaf Publishing*

Web: www.bookleafpub.com

E-mail: info@bookleafpub.com

ISBN: 9789360948030

First edition 2024

PREFACE

As I earned my Bachelor's and Master's degrees in Social Work, I began to realize the fundamental impact of unhealed trauma that individuals experience. I have become my own therapist, exploring and addressing the traumatic events that influenced how I showed up in the world. Becoming a healer has presented me with the gift of providing psychotherapy to individuals and families to promote addressing mental health.

Growing up in New York City, The Bronx, as a Malian Muslim woman, has motivated me to catch sight of my sense of self. Becoming whole has empowered me to strengthen my courage to get through life challenges. Being a mother to my two sons inspired me to strive for the best version of myself.

A painful experience encouraged me to start writing out my thoughts and emotions. Then I took heed in learning about poetry. I consistently started attending poetry shows and workshops. My devotion to being resilient and vulnerable has provided me the opportunity to create art for people to relate to. This book is for everyone who's struggling to overcome obstacles in life. This is my first piece of art and I hope to expand my work in aspiring others.

Thank you to my family and friends for supporting me throughout the hardships. Thank you for holding space for me while I gathered the pieces to establish my healing journey.

The Senses View

Look into my almond shape eyes
Deep into my mocha iris
Swim into my extraordinary pupil
Submerge yourself into the gateway of my
soul

See your reflection of burning desires
Feel the emotions of passion, not even water
can put out your fire
Taste the obsession of new waves coming
over you

Smell the scent of peppermints, it
invigorates the mind, if only you knew
Hear the ripple effects of your actions
impacting your mission
Feel unguarded boldness binding your
being with your every vision
See through every rain drop causing you to
look deeper in you
Taste the death of insecurity, let it go,
let it float away into a body of
bewilderment
Smell the adrenaline rushing across the
surface of your purpose
Hear the shallow calm peace over your
horizon

Gently, take your gaze away my from mine
Take a look into you
I mean…when it rains…it pours
Pour and pour into yourself until this is no
longer a preview,
more like the superior you…

Who Am I?

Her presence graciously commands a room
just as when a magician summons a
creature

Her skin melanated, kissed by the bronze
sun, every curve on her body blessed with
african goddess features

Her celestial voice is calming as the gentle
waves in the sea with unlimited measures

Her touches feel like cozy silk yet everyone
can't access it, it's expensive

A unique being formed by the Almighty as
he did with the beaming stars through only
his perspective

At times she's automatically viewed as an
bimbo yet intellect overflows with
discernment

Seems quiet as a mouse yet voice so mighty
when her inner lion roars

Genuine intentions, heart filled with love
and light, it's brighter than a pot of gold

Mishandled by the ones who mistreated her,
she who ignited love sparks only to be
burned by the fire

Conquering silent battles, gradually
overcoming adversities even if they're as
vast as the limitless sky

Aisse ASÈ

"AISSE" (ah-shay) be sure to say her name
Like when you say Asè
Let her name roll off your tongue
Her reawakening has begun

She is given the power of change, Asè
She had an epiphany that she won't dim her
lights
To let the others shine

She embodies the strength of a lion yet so
gentle like a
Soft breeze during summer nights

She exhibits wisdom while living life
young, wild, and free
She sets her past free, renouncing living in
misery's company

Her aura transcends through souls, without
saying a word…
She commands a room
Her walk exudes confidence, she only
acquires the best
Her love demands the highest level of active
healing,
It generates a deeper sense of feeling

She is the breath of fresh air, nonetheless
Her vengeance hurts like hell
She manifests and receives only because she
believes
Her trauma initiated rebirth to the point of
no return
She wears her scars graciously despite how
deep
Her wounds cut through her precious bones

Herstory, she rewrites…

She is Aisse, reborn and reformed through
The rebirth of self renewal,
But don't be misinformed
This course of action is limitless, infinite,
and boundless

Aisse, she is —

Asè

Freedom & Relief

She Screams, She Shouts
"LET ME OUT! LET ME GO!"
"I CAN'T TAKE THIS SHIT NO MORE!"

She fights and fights and still no freedom in
sight
Constantly being told she will always be the
prisoner…
being boxed in
All four corners are ignited with endless fire

She knows…that if she fights through this
fire
She will be burnt and everyday she
mourns…
She mourns until the day she is reborn
Indeed, she had burns
Burns that eventually healed with the
audacity of dignity
Initiating a divine Sense of Self

Thoughts and feelings of resilience generate
through her mind, body, and soul
But first she had to take control
Control of whether she will continue to be
held against her will
See that's no longer a fear
From that day forward, she wears
the scars of the burns as a testimony that
freedom is possible
Even when it's not permissible
She was unstoppable!!!

Now She Sings and Believes

"YOU WILL NEVER HOLD ME A
PRISONER AGAIN!"
"I REFUSE TO LOOSE MYSELF AT YOUR
EXPENSE!"

Pen's Moments

From the moment you reach out to hold me
I can sense dynamic words forming

From the moment, you let me glide across
your paper
I am automatically submissive, it's my
nature

There are many moments, many times,
When I feel like i'm having a seizure

I know you become excited to use me as
your vessel

Nonetheless, take it slow, and let your
thoughts settle
It's ok, I'll be your mind's temple

From the moment your exquisite hand grips
me
I know that you will become free
Whilst you will not feel any judgment from
me

From the moment you unhand me and store
me away until next time

Know that I will there with you to release
anything on your mind
Being that we are partners in crime

Yesterday, Today, & Tomorrow

Tomorrow is the unknown wonder of what
is yet to come…
Tomorrow leads one to believe it can be
done but not today, it's left unfulfilled
Tomorrow permits one to bargain the
commitment of today's dreams, time to
rebuild…
Tomorrow is not vowed, hone in on the
mission of today

Today is an opportunity to establish what
one wanted yesterday and tomorrow to
recreate
Today dictates whether one takes the steps
to embody the life one wishes to emulate
Today allows one to just start, not finish and
let it flow
Today is the present, let yesterday fade
away into the streams of letting go

Yesterday sanctioned misfortunes
Yesterday doesn't determine one's purpose
for certain
Yesterday has vanished, poof it's gone right
before one's eyes
Yesterday doesn't determine one's today
and tomorrow, it's a blessing in disguise…

Mama's Love for Two

Monica said it best
"I will cross the ocean for you, I will go and
bring you the moon."

Yes, you two
Hassan and Idris
Each born a prince
My SONshines
I will care for you two until my heart
flatlines
Allah created my babies with their own
special designs

Mama will always be in your corners
Mama believe in all of your superpowers

Idris and Hassan are original and unique as
the stars in the sky

I mean this with every cell in my body, even
after I die

Mama loves you two
When you two feel blue
Lay on my shoulders
I will bring you two closure

When you two feel alone
Remember you have Mama to call your
own
You two will always have a home
Know that Mama is always watching from
an imaginary drone

Monica said it best
"I will cross the ocean for you, I will go and
bring you the moon."

Mama's love will hold you two like a
cocoon.

Where Did the Pen Go?

Idris locked his nice pen in a hamper
Hassan enjoyed being a striker
They fought like Tom and Jerry
Then the hamper was empty

Hassan hid the pen in his diaper!

To My Past Self

A planted seed, who bloomed into the most
fascinating flower

Despite enduring unwarranted adversities,
this flower continued to blossom

Running through life living young, wild,
and free, sometimes…
unless that little flower was imposed to
make big decisions without any power

A planted seed, who bloomed into the most
fascinating flower

Nectar so sweet as honey and shiny as a
midnight star.
Scavengers would hunt however this flower
couldn't be devoured

The process of blooming and wilting
repeated itself
like when night transitions into day.
This resilient flower is the essence of
survival and wisdom

A planted seed, who bloomed into the most
fascinating flower

Despite enduring unwarranted adversities,
this flower continued to blossom

Cry

Cry…

With every single tear comes a story

It's that time when emotions that are feeling
unbearable

Whether it's silent like when time passes us
by, or yelling from the top of your lungs

Cry…

With every single tear comes a story

Whether sentiments of joy or wounds of
sorrow, here's a tissue you can borrow

Cry...

With every single tear comes a story

It's a way for your emotions to feel relief
while being released

To My Present Self

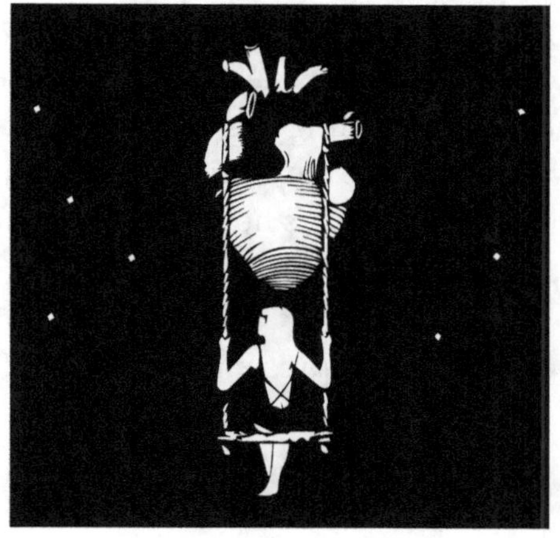

Within this present moment...

I'm at a loss for words, speechless

At this point in time I'm humbly blessed in every way, the Almighty has gifted me with pleasant presents

Within this present moment . . .

As a healer, I walk many pivotal paths with humankind in finding their way of catching

a breath of fresh air in the midst of
drowning in setbacks without judgment

Honoring the triumphs of victories, I
attained as a mother, sister, daughter, healer,
and wife. Recalling the very moments, I
would question my abilities while the
Almighty was always here with me whether
flawed or flawless

Within this present moment—

I'm at a loss for words, speechless

Happiness

Happiness…

We often focus on everything that is going wrong, if it's never nothing, it's always something. A thing that shifts our mood into endless doom

This great energy has to be founded within your soul. That responsibility isn't an obligation of someone outside of yourself.

It's up to you for your happiness to be
determined

Finding joy in things
as little as waking up and catching your
first breath for the day,
or something as big as you can imagine

Happiness…

It's more than a feeling, it's a way of living
Feels like walking on air
even when there's misery happening all
around you

We often focus on everything that is going
wrong, if it's never nothing, it's always
something. A thing that shifts our mood
into endless doom

Did you know happiness really starts with
you? …Boom!

To My Future Self

Who knows what lies ahead…

For my future, I anticipate embodying my full potential of becoming my true self

Life will be successful even with hurdles of obstacles.
Creating harmony amongst the highs and lows. Finding balance within like a needle and thread.

Who knows what lies ahead…

There will not be any tolerance of acts I
don't believe in. Grace will be given to
myself instead

Refusing to let my past dictate my future.
Placing my needs and wants on a pedestal
in the face of the life that I have been dealt

Who knows what lies ahead…

For my future, I anticipate embodying my
full potential of becoming my true self

W.O.M.S

The Weight on My Shoulders

Weights of his unceasing burdens feels like
a chokehold

On every inhale of a new breath, the exhale
ends before it begins

My existence is centered around coddling
his shortcomings. "Be his peace," does that
mean to surrender every piece of me?

Especially to the aches of my chest and shoulders?

Shoulders are no longer used to convey confidence, conviction, and courage more so a pedestal of bearing the burdens for him to feel safe and sound without any bounds…

I Choose ME

I choose ME
and I will choose me every time
Because you chose not to choose me
I am left to only choose me

Choosing me means…
Choosing my sons' emotional and mental
sanity
Choosing me means…
Choosing to stand by my values
Choosing me means…
Choosing to honor my worth

I chose to own my today and tomorrow
Choosing you to stay within my yesterday

I choose to no longer choose you
Therefore I must,

Choose ME

Eeny, Meeny, Miny, Moe ...

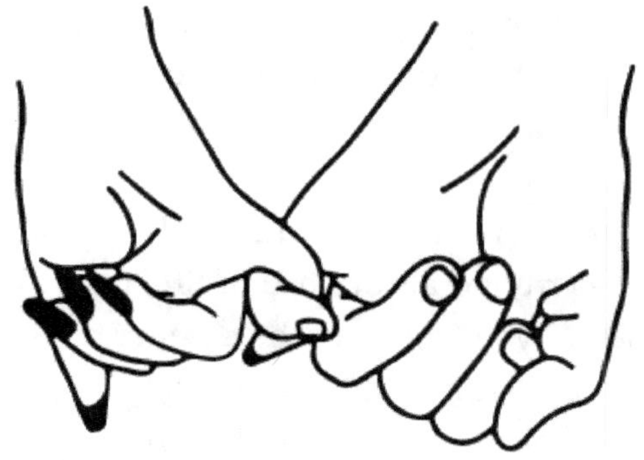

Eeny, Meeny, Miny, Moe…
Catch these men by their toes
Bound to choose the one I want, I suppose
Don't hate the player, that's the way the
game goes

Eeny, Meeny, Miny, Moe ...
and if he hollers, let him go
I won't settle, after all I will reap what I sow
Have my options open and keep em close

Eeny, Meeny, Miny, Moe…

I always abide by my standards, no I don't
just go with the flow
Don't want it, if we can't grow
Fuck potential, I refuse to let him string me
along and not propose

Eeny, Meeny, Miny… No !
See my petals are full of life, he will
definitely be chosen if he doesn't treat me
like a dried up rose
And if he's everything and more, trust me I
will know
Once my king is in my possession, I will be
addicted to only him…like a drug dose

A Life Sentence

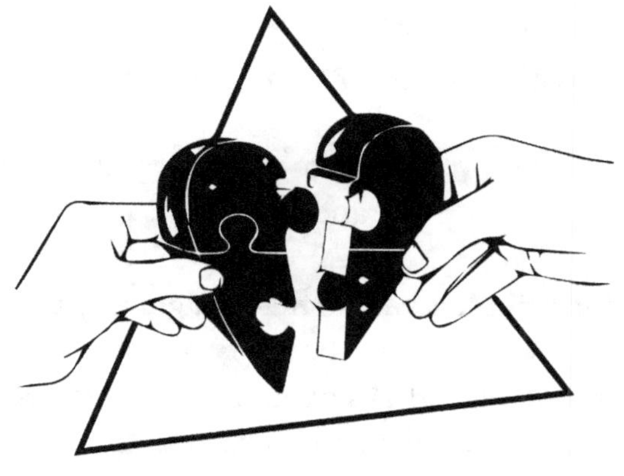

I didn't intend to love you yet you loved me
purposely…wholeheartedly

My heart was telling me yes but my mind
was telling me — "No!"

I didn't know which way to go, it was too
much sauce in your flow

A chapter was created in a book I was
hesitant to read

Is this really meant to be? We were growing
like a seed

Really didn't want my heart to be broken

I couldn't look away, because your gaze
locked into mine, and you had me open!

Who would've known we go together like
salt and pepper

I don't think love like this can get any better

His touch is light as a feather yet he loves so
hard with so much pressure

Finally, I allow myself to give love and to be
loved, no longer will I feel numb

It's the way you consume me with your
presence…
now I'm stuck to you like a life sentence

A.F.R.I.C.A.N.I.S.T

A.F.R.I.C.A.N.I.S.T

A
Future's
Righteous
Inheritance
Ceased although retrieved
Ambition we achieved
Nuances of fortitude
Influences of ancestry
Shades of legendary heritage
Till the end we'll stay linked to our lineage

A Sister Who is Your Best Friend

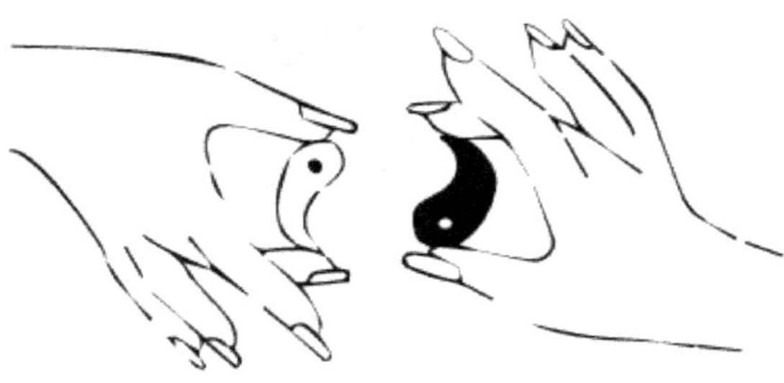

I have the best sister in the whole wide
world
Wouldn't trade her for anything, that's
absurd

We laugh, cry, fight all the time, even
known as partners in crime
I can even be my full authentic self without
being judged by her
We're great at tango-ing through life
together like we do on any dance floor

She sees the best in me before I do
She is a significant piece to my puzzle

She's unique, genuine, brilliant,
and let's not forget resilient.

Most of all she's special…

Special is even an understatement, she's an
empress full of exceptional wisdom. With
quite honesty, the girls cannot even be on
her level.

Furthermore, our kids call each of us their
mommy!
I am grateful to have gone through the most
difficult times of my life with you, I don't
think I would be who I am today without
you.

My sister, my best friend, my partner in
crime, my ride or die.
I truly do love you
Jennabou!

The End Of Sun

From sunrise to sunset
From dawn to dusk
From today night will fall and there will be
no day
No prosperity of sun rays

No longer will I glide through the skies
No longer will I bless my array of sunshine
Upon the surface of the earth
No longer will my shine give birth
From the plants, down to the dirt
No way down to the roots, even the fruits

Beings of humanity will no longer feel my
Warmth to keep them safe

Safe emotionally, physically, and
Most of all… mentally
My light beams so bright
Even a million diamonds and I aren't alike
I am one of a kind

Not a galaxy, planet, moon, star
Will longer feel the beam of my light of day
It all ends today

I, the sun is meant to set one last time
Now it's time for my goodbye

Resurrection

Life can be full of readjustments
They say…expectations lead to
disappointments
Like when your feelings of hope are being
beaten by a pipe with spikes

They say…there's light at the end of the
tunnel, don't you dare give a rebuttal!
Any loss of hope gives a sense of death,
then you have no more breaths

They say…there will be sunshine after the
rain
See that's what rebirth feels like
let me explain…
Be the rebirth of your whole being, it's a
part of healing

Continue to have those expectations until
they are fulfilled…
even in the midst of disappointments
I mean it's about perception

I say it's like a…Resurrection

www.ingramcontent.com/pod-product-compliance
Lightning Source LLC
LaVergne TN
LVHW010826200726

843508LV00012B/2507